Slum Life in Edinburgh, or, Scenes in Its Darkest Places

SLUM LIFE
IN EDINBURGH

With
Twelve
ustrations
from
Life

𝔈𝔡𝔦𝔫𝔟𝔲𝔯𝔤𝔥

JAMES THIN

SCOTTISH NATIONAL SOCIETY

FOR THE

Prevention of Cruelty to Children.

PRESIDENT | *PATRONESS*
H.R.H. THE PRINCE OF WALES.   **H.R.H. THE DUCHESS OF FIFE.**

DIRECTORS OF EASTERN DISTRICT.

Vice-Presidents—

Ex-Bailie COLSTON, J.P.   **General NEPEAN SMITH.**

Colonel AGNEW, JOSEPH BELL, M.D., P.R.C.S ; W. S. BROWN,
JAMES CARMICHAEL, M D.; Rev. J. G. CUNNINGHAM, General GRANT,
R. C. GRAY, Rev. ANDREW KEAY, HENRY D. LITTLEJOHN, M.D.;
JAMES M'INTOSH, CLAUD MUIRHEAD, M.D., F.R.C.P.; Rev. P. C.
PURVES, R. L. STUART, Rev. C. R. TEAPE, D.D.; JOHN USHER, Rev.
GEORGE WILSON, Rev. J. S WILSON, DAVID E. YOUNG.

SHELTER—150 HIGH STREET.

*Matron—*Miss STEPHEN.

CHILDREN'S HOME—MURRAYFIELD.

*Matron—*Mrs WALKER.

*Lady Superintendent—*Miss SUTTER.

*Officer—*JOHN M'INTYRE.

All communications referring to Cruelty to Children should
be addressed to the Secretary, 3A Pitt Street.

Contributions of Clothing (Old and New), Boots, Shoes, Toys,
Provisions, &c., gratefully received. As the children's clothes
have usually to be burnt when they are first brought to the
Shelter, clothing is in great demand. Parcels will be sent for
on receipt of post-card

Funds are urgently needed. Subscriptions and Donations
received and acknowledged by the

Honorary Secretary and Treasurer,

JOHN MACDONALD, 3A PITT STREET.

SLUM LIFE IN EDINBURGH.

PREFACE.

...ESE sketches were first printed in the ...EKLY SCOTSMAN, and strongly excited the ...ntion of the Public. So many suggestions ...publish them in book form were made to me, ...t I now do so in the hope that their publi-...ion may be of some little use to those who ...striving to solve the great problem of the age.

EDINBURGH, 1891.

SLUM LIFE

IN EDINBURGH

OR

SCENES IN ITS DARKEST PLACES

BY

T. B. M.

WITH TWELVE ILLUSTRATIONS FROM LIFE

EDINBURGH: JAMES THIN
1891

LIST OF ILLUSTRATIONS.

CONTENTS.

————

SLUM LIFE IN EDINBURGH.

I.

THE POOR MAN AT HOME.

WE are no "Special Commissioners" deputed to paint lurid pictures of slum horrors; we are not sentimental slummers who run hither and thither in the search for social sores over which to gush and weep; we see no reason for abusing the authorities, or the administrators of public or private charities; we do not even cherish a theory, the carrying out of which would secure the salvation of the "submerged tenth." We simply wish, in these articles, to draw a few unexaggerated pictures, or rather sketches, of the conditions under which the inhabitants of those lower regions exist; to tell something of their homes and their mode of life, their struggles and their sufferings, with which we have become acquainted in the course of long wanderings among the courts and closes and back streets of the city.

This, we believe, is not yet a work of super-
erogation; for, notwithstanding all that has been
said and written of the poorer classes, the quarters
where they congregate are still "dark places" to
all but a comparative few. To the vast majority
the "one-roomed house," the squalor and destitution of the poor, are but the merest abstractions,
or are vaguely associated with notorious East
End localities. It is only when we come face
to face with the misery itself, instead of con-
fining our knowledge to that derived from the
reports of charitable institutions, that we can
realise its awful actuality.

We need not travel four hundred miles to
Whitechapel; we have a Whitechapel at our
own doors, gruesome enough to satisfy the
cravings of the sensation hunter, big enough
to absorb all our time, money, and philanthropic zeal.

A walk through the Grassmarket or Cowgate,
or down the Lawnmarket and Canongate, is at
times a very depressing experience; but one
has to explore the huge tenements that tower
on either side of the street, to enter the houses
and speak with the people, to arrive at an
adequate idea of what life in some parts of the
slums means. A night spent in such an ex-

ploration—climbing foul and rickety stairs, grop-
ing your way along a network of dark, narrow
passages, and peering into the dismal dens which
the wretched inhabitants (and their landlords)
call "houses"—a night passed in this manner
will give an experience of horrors that will for
ever remain imprinted on the memory.

Go into any one of the courts in the Lawnmarket, for instance; glance up at the rows of
windows, and then reflect for a minute or two.
Windows everywhere—looking to front, to back,
into courts and closes; and each one of them
probably represents a "one-roomed house," inhabited by from two to eight or nine persons.
The rooms, once the spacious chambers of the
aristocracy of Edinburgh, have been partitioned
off into small box-like apartments, like the cells
of a honeycomb. Everybody is familiar with the
filth of the closes and courts: these, then, need
not be further described. The stairs are in a
corresponding state of foulness. The seemingly
interminable passages which penetrate in all
directions into these human warrens are narrow,
and in general very badly lighted; in many the
darkness seems almost to be palpable, so dense is
it. Along these corridors the doors of the rooms
are ranged within a few feet of each other. A

close, sickening odour pervades the passages. It is an indescribable smell—a compound of all the foul vapours escaping from numberless reeking hovels. Sometimes when you enter a room, fumes like the quintessence of all villainous smells combined, make you gasp, and then, rushing down to the very foundations of your vitals, cause a sensation as if the stomach were trying to turn a somersault. But conquering an instinctive desire to shut the door and beat a retreat, you enter the room and look around you.

The room, for which a weekly rent of from one and threepence to half-a-crown is paid, is small, dirty, and dingy. The walls are black with the smoke and dirt of years; here and there the plaster has fallen off in patches, and reveals the laths beneath. The floor looks as if soap and water were still unknown in these regions; likewise the crazy deal table—if there happens to be one. There may be a chair with a decayed back, but frequently a roughly-made stool or an upturned box does duty instead. And the bed! These lairs—for the word "bed" may suggest erroneous ideas of luxury—have long been a marvel to us; inasmuch as it is difficult to imagine how blankets, which presumably were once white, have assumed a hue so dark. They appear to have been steeped in a solution of soot and water—blankets, pillows, and mattress, or what stand for such. Generally the bed is a wooden one, a venerable relic of bygone fashions, bought for a trifle from the furniture broker on the other side of the street. But very often a bedstead is not included in the furnishings of the chamber, in which case the family couch consists of a mattress or a bundle of rags, or some straw laid in the least draughty corner of the room, and covered over with any kind of rags that can be gathered together.

There a whole family will lie down at night, and when the cold is intense, and the piercing wind whistles through the chinks in the window frames, right glad they are to huddle together for the sake of warmth. It is no uncommon thing to see five or six, or even seven, persons in one bed—father, mother, and four or five children, one foetid intertwined mass of humanity. The unspeakably horrible results of this over-crowding need not be described; they can be readily imagined. For it is not only children who are packed together within the four walls of one chamber. It is quite a usual thing to find grown-up people herding together in one small room, without any pretence of privacy or decency.

SLUM LIFE

IN EDINBURGH

OR

SCENES IN ITS DARKEST PLACES

BY

T. B. M.

WITH TWELVE ILLUSTRATIONS FROM LIFE

.

EDINBURGH: JAMES THIN

1891

PREFACE.

THESE sketches were first printed in the WEEKLY SCOTSMAN, and strongly excited the attention of the Public. So many suggestions to publish them in book form were made to me, that I now do so in the hope that their publication may be of some little use to those who are striving to solve the great problem of the age.

EDINBURGH, 1891.

In a room in the Lawnmarket we found a man and his wife in bed, both unwell. The husband had been out of health and unable to work for twelve months, and he and his wife were supported by a daughter of twenty years of age, who earned seven shillings and sixpence a week, and shared their room, *and their bed*, with them. And they would think you had queer notions if you expressed surprise at this natural arrangement.

Another room—this one in the Castle Wynd—presented a scene that is only too easily paralleled in any part of our slums. It was typical of the poor man's home. The room was filthy beyond description. From the blackened walls the paper hung in shreds, and in one corner the damp had discoloured the plaster beyond the power of whitewash to restore. A feeble light from a paraffin lamp shed its melancholy rays over a group of two men, two girls, and a boy cowering round a cinder fire which they were in vain endeavouring to coax into a flame. Beside them, on a bundle of rags on the floor, lay a woman and two grown-up daughters; and on a decrepit bedstead, curled up among a few foul cloths that no one would think of calling bed-clothes, a man was sleeping off the effects of a two-days' carouse.

JL. Veitch

A HOVEL IN LOWER GREENSIDE.

In this dark, damp den, the weekly rent of which was two shillings and fourpence, the man, his wife, and five children, the eldest of whom was a girl of eighteen, lived—under what conditions we shall leave the reader to depict for himself.

But this is almost a desirable residence compared with some of the abodes that may be seen any day of the week. In Lower Greenside, where there are some execrable specimens of one-roomed houses, we stumbled across a den about twelve feet square. It was a debateable point which was the more hideous, the room or its occupants. Furniture there was none, unless a shakedown of rags, a stool, and an empty orange box may go by that name. In the grate an old boot was burning, for the supply of cinders had run out. On one side of the fire sat an unkempt virago, with a baby at her breast and a pipe in her mouth. Opposite to her crouched an aged woman, whose grey dishevelled hair, hooked nose, and brown, minutely wrinkled face gave her a very witch-like appearance. Cross-legged between them sat a boy of about ten years of age. This beldam, having reached the sive stage of intoxication, was venting her spleen in a shower of oaths and curses upon her companion with the baby and the pipe : but the latter treated her volleys of vituperation with the calmness bred of use and wont ; only at intervals removing her pipe from her mouth and commanding the old woman to " shut up," an injunction always followed by a fierce, complicated oath.

A feature of this low life that impresses one with painful vividness is the total absence of anything approaching rational enjoyment or employment. When a man in comfortable circumstances goes home from his day's work, he generally finds a cheery hearth and a warm meal awaiting him. Then, if he does not go out for a walk, or to visit friends, or to some place of entertainment, he puts his slippered feet on the fender and has his pipe and his newspaper ; or, if he is a family man, he enjoys the company of his wife and children. At all events he is fed and warm, and his mind is more or less at ease.

The forlorn being of whom we write returns to the hovel he calls his home, after, it may be, a day spent in a fruitless search for work. He finds nothing there to cheer or attract him. Dirt and desolation everywhere ! His better-half not remarkable for her tidiness. A swarm of ragged, hungry bairns are sprawling about the

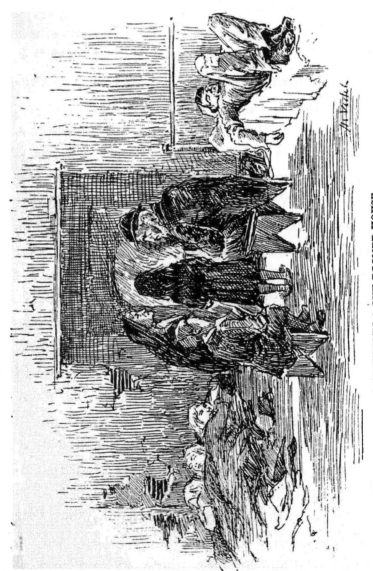

A FAMILY IN A ONE-ROOMED HOUSE.

floor. It depends on chance and the luck of the day whether there is any supper or not. Possibly there is not a crust in the house. Though the night is bitterly cold, there is only a handful of smouldering cinders in the grate, and a chillness that penetrates to the very marrow pervades the room. Books or newspapers he has none; probably he could not read them if he had any. The night is too cold for loafing at the "close-mouth"—a favourite summer pastime of our slum denizens; so all he can do is to kill time till he shuffles off to bed.

It sickens the heart to see the hopeless, aimless demeanour of a family group such as this. There they sit, as close to the meagre fire as possible; gloomy emptiness on all sides. They do nothing; of conversation they have little, only an occasional remark is dropped in a listless way. When one surprises a household in this attitude, he is impressed with the idea that this cluster of silent figures are expecting something—waiting for something to turn up. But if they are expectant, it is of something that never comes. At length, hungry, shivering, utterly wretched, they throw themselves upon the pallet of straw and rags, and for a time forget their misery in sleep.

II.

STARVING IN SILENCE.

IT is the impudent beggar who hustles to the front, and carries off the lion's share of Charity's doles. He never starves. He is too 'cute ever to fall into such dire extremity. If the calamity he dreads most of all comes upon him, and he is actually compelled to exert himself to keep body and soul together, he knows how to do so with the minimum of trouble and the maximum of profit to himself. With all the outs and ins of the " moucher's " life he is familiar, and he is unconcerned ; for he is assured that in this city of many charities his wants will not go long unrelieved. Assistance can be got for the asking : why, therefore, should he so far forget himself as to render unnecessary the offices of the good Samaritans ?

It is needless to say that this rascal does not belong to the silent, suffering class. At all points he is dissimilar to him who is known as the " deserving " poor man. The latter is honest and clings to his independence. He is probably a labourer or in one of the lower grades of artisans. But, notwithstanding all his endeavours, the nature of his calling is such that he for ever lives on the borderland of destitution. His wages are so small and his family so large that it is only by severe pinching that both ends are made to meet. There is nothing laid by for a rainy day; and when a temporary slackness or dislocation of trade throws him out of employment, he and his family at once begin to feel the grip of poverty.

Such a man is very often quite ignorant of the ways of obtaining charitable aid. So long as he is able-bodied the Parochial Board will not give him outdoor relief, and he has a horror of "the House." There is thus nothing between him and slow starvation; and he drags through weeks in silent hunger, parting with his furniture bit by bit, until the tide of fortune turns, and he once again finds work to support himself and his family. And in this manner he passes his life, in continual oscillation between bare sufficiency and sheer starvation.

Winter is the time dreaded most by these hard-tried creatures, for then outdoor work is uncertain. Should a slackness in trade be added to inclement weather, then their lot is pitiable in the extreme. During the recent railway strike, for instance, the sufferings of the labouring classes were intense. It was not the railway men who suffered; it was those who had been employed in works dependent on the railway for supplies. Their name was legion. In the course of the strike we personally discovered scores of families rendered utterly destitute by this means. One case we shall describe as a typical one.

In a wretched hovel, a mere corner of a room, we came upon a young man, with his wife and two infants. Their appearance and scant surroundings indicated only too clearly abject poverty. When we entered, the man was in bed ; on the coverlet sat one of the children crying in a faint, weary voice ; and the woman, pale, thin, and wan, sat over the fireless hearth, " crooning " the other infant to sleep. The scene was one of dull, settled despair. This desolation notwithstanding, the faces and the bearing of the young couple bore the unmistakable stamp of respectability. They were not of the coarse, brutal mould in which their squalid neighbours were cast ; and, unlike them, they were not ready to pour forth the tale of their sufferings. But questioning brought out a pitiable tale.

Till the time of the strike they had lived in a small but comfortable house of two rooms in a comparatively respectable locality. But the strike threw the man idle, and in a little more than a week they were forced to leave their house and to take refuge in the miserable den we found them in. There, to add to their misfortunes, the man was seized with rheumatism and had to take to bed. The young woman, unacquainted with the method of obtaining parochial relief, and apparently loth to avail herself of such assistance, sold the furniture bit by bit until the barest necessaries only were left. Then they began to experience absolute starvation. It was a Thursday night when we saw them, and the father and mother had not tasted any food since the Wednesday morning except a half-penny bran scone; while a single biscuit between them was all the nourishment that the children had got. Certainly the haggard, hunger-bitten appearance of the family bore out the truth of the statement. During the preceding fortnight not a soul had entered the door, saving a well-intentioned elderly lady, who had called one Sunday and left a religious tract—not a very satisfying allowance among four starving mortals.

This was a case of starving respectability. But

when starvation is found hand in hand with filth and rags, the effect produced upon the observer is almost staggering.

One night, on chancing to open the door of a room in a Cowgate close, an involuntary exclamation of horror escaped our lips. It was a small apartment, in size about three strides either way, in the last stages of decay. The walls were brown with dirt. A dirty bedstead, covered with a few clothes in a state of filth harmonising with the general foulness of the room, stood in one corner; a tumble-down table was propped up in another; and through the smoke that filled the room we could indistinctly see, huddling round the fire, the raggedest and dirtiest group of human beings we ever set eyes on.

Seated on rude benches round the fire, stretching out their hands greedily towards the feeble flames, were a man and his wife, a girl of about ten years of age, and two boys of younger age; and in a box resembling a cradle lay an infant of a few weeks. The boys were tattered enough in all conscience; one of them had on only a fragmentary shirt, and lower garments many sizes too large for him, suspended by a single brace. But as a picturesque raggamuffin he was entirely cast into the shade by his sister. Her face had upon it the accumulated dirt of weeks; her dishevelled hair had long been innocent of the comb; part of the skirt of an old dress was thrown over her shoulders, and a rag of indefinite shape and origin was tied round her waist. There was nothing between these worn-out shreds and her bare skin, as her father demonstrated by drawing aside the rags and uncovering the dirt-engrained body.

This was a case of terrible destitution. There was not a morsel of food in the house, and no prospect of getting any. The father, a mason's labourer, had been disabled by an accident to his leg three weeks before, and was unable to work. During that time they had received half-a-crown a week from the Parochial Board; but it will be allowed that five sixpences a week are starvation rations for a family of six souls. The eagerness of these poor creatures at the mention of bread was touching to behold. The small boy fairly tumbled down the stair after us in his hurry to get the loaf we purchased at a neighbouring shop.

Appalling as was this picture of want and wretchedness, it was surpassed in gruesomeness by an experience we had in another hovel in Covenant Close, High Street. The room was like many others in that locality—small, ill-ventilated,

dirty to the last degree, and in a state of miserable disrepair. Though the night was one of the
coldest we had this winter, there was no fire, and
from the mantelshelf a lamp in which the oil was
all but exhausted, gave out a flickering light that
served only to reveal the wretchedness of the surroundings. A broken chair stood by the cheerless
hearth, and this was all the furniture with the exception of a bed, in which, wrapped in ragged
blankets, lay a pale-faced, un-washed boy. But
it was the appearance of the woman who opened
the door that struck us with a feeling akin to
horror. She was literally half naked. Her feet
were bare ; a short, tattered gown scarce covered
the calves of her legs ; her dress, open at the neck,
showed her grimy breast, and round her head was
bound a scrap of flannel, with which she tried to
assuage the pangs of neuralgia. Neuralgia under
the most advantageous circumstances is torture
enough ; what it must have been with the added
pains of hunger and cold would baffle the power
of language to describe.

This woman's story was short, and as grievous as
short. Her husband, a labourer, was idle, thrown
out of work by the railway strike. At that
moment he was out searching for employment.
She had no money, no food, no coal, no oil for the

lamp, and was just about to huddle in beside her child for the sake of the little warmth the scanty blankets could afford. She was ill and starving, but it was needless to tell us that. The ghastly figure before us told its own tale without words. We gave the woman a little money to stave off starvation a little longer, and then left this grim chamber of horrors. From a neighbour we learned that the poor creature had been apprehended by the police that morning for stealing a piece of coal, but that the authorities, evidently moved with compassion at her pitiable plight, had detained her in the cells for only three hours, and then set her free to go "home." One is inclined to think that, under the circumstances, freedom was not a thing to be desired.

Such privation as this could not be of long duration; in whatever way it ended it must of necessity be sharp and short. Less startling, it may be, but every whit as saddening, are the cases of chronic destitution which are found with distressing frequency in one's wanderings in the slums. Away down in those sunless, joyless regions there are hundreds of hapless beings who, even by incessant toil, cannot keep their heads above water. They do not know what it is to have a short respite from anxiety for their next meal.

They seldom experience the satisfaction of having a full meal; hunger is ever their companion. In the hovels of Lower Greenside may be found not a few instances of poor families whom stress of circumstances has driven from comfortable and respectable homes. The true blatant, brutal slum "moucher" born and bred is indigenous to the Cowgate and the Grassmarket, and the adjacent localities; but, so far as we could judge, Lower Greenside hides within its sombre depths a different class of people—unfortunate creatures of undoubted respectability who have been forced to retreat step by step before their gaunt enemy Poverty, until at length they found themselves immured in those dismal subterraneous regions.

A case illustrative of this gradual descent was that of a seamstress, who lived in a room there with her two children. Though she was yet under middle age, her face was worn and deeply lined, while her haggard, anxious face and bent figure told of a hard struggle for existence. Once she had been better off, her husband being a tailor in good employment. But he died, and she supported herself and her two children by working as a machinist. Soon, however, her eyesight, which had never been of the best, began to fail. Day after day brought increasing diffi-

A STARVING SEAMSTRESS AT WORK.

culty; she struggled against the infirmity; but eventually she lost her situation, for she was unable to do the fine work demanded of her. Now she kept body and soul together by doing odd dressmaking jobs where careful workmanship was not necessary, such as repairing or making down an old dress for any of her poor neighbours. In this way, and by doing such charing as she could get, she made from half-a-crown to three and sixpence a week, and even this wretched pittance was precarious. This was all she had with which to pay her rent of one and sixpence a week, and to provide food, coal, and oil. Indeed, she said, were it not for an occasional soup ticket and scraps of food given to her by tender-hearted neighbours almost as poor as herself, she could not live at all, for often she was entirely without food or money, and did not know where her next meal was to come from.

She had applied to the Parochial Board, but had been refused assistance, because she lived in a "land" which had an evil repute, and the parochial authorities are naturally chary of giving relief to persons whom they suspect of leading an immoral life. Could she, then, not remove to a respectable locality? But here she was confronted with an insurmountable difficulty. To remove, money was necessary, for she could not get another house unless she paid the landlord a month's rent in advance, which is the invariable rule with the proprietors of those one-roomed houses. A month's rent meant six shillings, and to her six shillings was a great sum of money, quite beyond her power to scrape together.

And thus she remained, chained to the rock; toiling in hunger and squalor for her forty pence a week, and glad that by so doing she could keep her bairns with her in that dilapidated and almost furnitureless shelter.

These are mere sketches of scenes whose hideousness can only be realised when viewed at close quarters, and the contemplation of which produces a sense of helplessness bordering upon despair. You may do your best to relieve a hungering family here and there, but you do so with the feeling that you might as well try to dip the ocean dry with a teaspoon. And yet the public seem to have the comfortable notion that though the poor of Edinburgh have their hard times like other people, they rarely suffer from actual starvation. This is a reasonable belief when one considers the huge sum that is spent in charitable objects; but, nevertheless, the public are labouring under a sad delusion.

DRIVEN TO THE STREETS.

III.

THE CRY OF THE CHILDREN.

AT every turn in an exploration of the slums, one has his emotions of pity, or despair, or indignation aroused; but there is nothing that so thoroughly melts the heart to compassion, or depresses it to hopelessness, or fills it to bursting-point with hot indignation, as an insight into the conditions under which the children of the poor exist. Pity for the wretched lot of a man or a woman is almost always tempered with the reflection that they have their fate in their own hands, and that they probably have themselves been partly to blame for their degraded state. But there is no such consideration to mitigate the flow of sympathy for the hapless bairns, of whom it may be said without exaggeration that they have been "damned, not born into the world." They might almost as well have been born in hell so far as their chances of virtuous rearing are concerned.

Let fathers and mothers who have comfortable

homes filled with bright-eyed children consider the constant watchfulness, care, and tenderness they must exercise to keep alive and train their offspring—and this with all the advantages of decent surroundings, a sufficient income, and healthy moral influences. Let them first ponder these things, and then let them turn to look upon child-life in the slums, and they will soon cease to wonder why there is so much poverty, misery, and crime in the city.

If medical men whose duties take them to these dark regions would speak, they could tell facts that would make one shudder; and not the least horrifying of these would be of the manner in which many of the children of the poor are ushered into the world.

It is not an unusual thing on the eve of a birth for a supply of whisky to be brought in to celebrate the event. The father and a few neighbours with a keen scent for the liquor gather in the room where the woman is lying. The whisky is produced, and a preliminary " nip " goes round. Naturally this is followed by another and another, till the guests become noisy; more drink is sent for, and the tippling quickly develops into a riotous drinking bout.

Picture the horrors of such a scene; a woman

lying in agony in the midst of a drunken, cursing crew, too intoxicated to listen to or understand her cries of pain. A doctor tells us that on one occasion when called to an accouchement he found the room like a piggery; the husband, in a state of bestial intoxication, lay snoring on the floor; and three half-clothed women in an advanced stage of befuddlement were huddled together in one corner of the room. In another case the husband, who was fighting drunk, loudly swore that he would not allow the doctor to lay a finger upon his wife, who lay bleeding to death from internal hemorrhage. The doctor had to get the infuriated man removed before he could turn his attention to the dying woman.

A third instance, surpassing these in ghastliness of detail, was given to us by a woman who at one time was a manageress in a lodging-house. A woman, one of the lodgers, and among the most abandoned of the lot, was about to be delivered. A day or two before the birth she "got on the spree" with several companions. She happened to be one of those bedevilled beings, who, when once set agoing, never stop drinking till they have not a copper, or a bit of furniture or scrap of clothing that can be converted into money. So at it they went. First

their money was spent; then the few shillings'
worth of furniture was liquidated; the baby-
clothes lent to her by a neighbour went next,
to be followed soon by the blankets off the bed
on which the woman about to become a mother
lay.   At length these insatiable drunkards took
the very clothes off the woman, every rag of
them, and pawned them to get whisky.   Whether
they did this last with or without the consent of
the woman we do not know; but this, we were
assured, was a fact: when the doctor came he
found the woman lying stark naked on the bare
mattress, and when the child was born it had to
be wrapped in a piece of an old sack.   Having
attended to the babe, the doctor went away, and
returned soon after with blankets and some
human-like clothing for the infant.

So much for the way in which these little
creatures of the slums first see the light.

Their upbringing is in keeping with this initial
stage; or, to speak more correctly, they have no
upbringing, they are merely left to "hang as they
grow," surrounded by every manner of abomina-
tion.   Born amidst debauchery and blasphemy,
their infancy is passed in neglect and privation,
unless, happily for themselves, they go to swell
the numbers of our enormous infant mortality.

Even set down in cold figures, the mortality
among this class of children is startling enough—
over fifty per cent. of the whole number of deaths
in the poor quarters of the town, compared with
eight per cent. among the children of the upper
classes. In other words, of the total number of
deaths in one-roomed dwellings, one half is set
down to infant mortality ; while of the deaths
that take place in houses rented above £30, not
a twelfth are those of children of five years and
under. What a hideous revelation of the suffering and criminal neglect by which those innocents
are done to death ! For they cannot be said to
die from " natural causes."

In an evil-smelling room, a mere closet, in a
Cowgate tenement, we found three women and
two men, who were evidently in the course of
enjoying a prolonged " boose." On a filthy bed
two children were lying, ill with the whooping-
cough. They were not *in* the bed ; the unfeeling
mother had carelessly laid them, with their clothes
on, on the top of the blankets. It was plain that
one of the children, an infant about six months
old, was on the point of death. It lay on its
back breathing in gasps, with livid face, and
its thin little arms extended in front of it in a
most unnatural position, as if they were already

c

stiffening.   And yet, while the bairns were thus
suffering, the men and women scarcely took any
notice of them.   Half-dazed with drink, they
were waiting for the return of one of their
number with whisky from the public house at
the foot of the stair.   A few minutes after we
quitted this wretched hovel there issued from it
the sounds of cursing and fighting, followed by
a heavy thud on the floor, as of two persons
falling together in a struggle, and a string of
frightful oaths were ground out from between
clenched teeth.   The division of the whisky
had apparently led to a fight; and though
the whole landing rang with the hullabaloo,
not one of the inhabitants paid the slightest
attention to it.   These scenes are too common
to attract attention.

To such a life the slum-born child awakens to
consciousness.   Its first impressions are of reeling
parents, drunken brawls, and every kind of brut-
ality and indecency.   Its first lisping attempts at
speech are mingled with the oaths and foulness
that enter into the every-day conversation of its
elders.   One is shocked to notice the utter disregard of the men and women for decency of
speech in the presence of children.   Blackguards
of the better classes usually restrain themselves

if young people happen to be present, but not
so their fellow-roughs of the lower strata of
society. Among them oaths and the filthiest
of language are bandied about without regard
to age or sex; and, naturally, the children
imitate their language and actions. Morality
has no chance of life in such a pestilential
atmosphere. These are, indeed, regions "where
virtue is impossible, and goodness a dream of
an unknown land."

The size of the poor man's family has long been
proverbial, and one striking, and at the same time
distressing, feature of this side of slum-life is the
great number of children that one sees. They
swarm everywhere—lying asleep in coils in the
dreary rooms; loitering aimlessly about in the
dark passages; or disporting themselves in the
courts and streets as only street arabs can.
Picture to yourself the squalid misery of a one-
roomed dwelling filled with tattered, hungry
children, to whose wail for bread the helpless
mother can only reply with vague promises of
food which her own aching heart tells her are
but fencings with despair.

A scene like this we came upon in the dusk of
a cold winter day. The mother, a hollow-cheeked,
famine-worn woman, was pacing the room singing

softly to an infant in her arms, while the second youngest of her seven bairns held her skirts and whimpered for bread. The other five, the eldest of whom was barely twelve years of age, were crouching round a dispirited-looking fire. With the exception of a bed there was not a single article of furniture in the room—not a table, not a chair, not even a stool or a box on which to take a seat. This destitute family were waiting for the father to come home; he was out of work and had been away all day searching for employment.

We leave to others to explain *why* it generally falls to the lot of poor men to accumulate large families, contenting ourselves with the observation that their improvidence has certainly the support of their affluent fellow-men. By our system of charity we place a premium on thriftlessness and irresponsibility. The careless parent regards his increasing family without concern, for he knows that the maintenance of his children will not press upon him as a very heavy burden. They will be educated for nothing; odds and ends of clothing given by some charitable society or philanthropic individual will serve to cover their nakedness; and as for food, they can rub along pretty well with what they may get at soup kitchens and " free breakfasts," or may pick up in the streets;

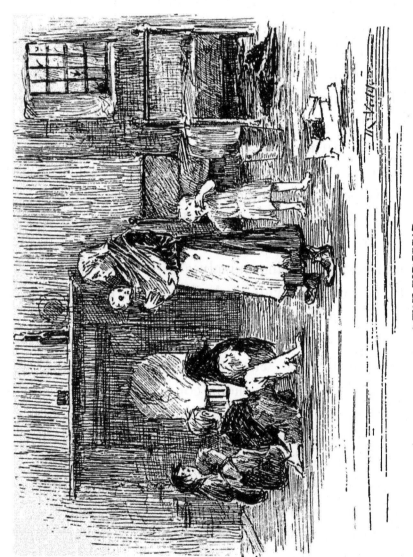

A WAIL FOR BREAD.

and what does he care for their sufferings so long as they do not cost him anything and he is left to go comfortably to the devil? And so they are practically turned adrift on the world.

How these waifs contrive to exist is a mystery. The "hardening" theory is the only explanation; for their sufferings are awful to contemplate; it is almost impossible to fall into exaggeration in describing them. They are neglected, starved, beaten. The brute who begot them frequently exhausts his drunken fury upon them for any reason or for none. Then they flee in terror from him into the streets, and, not knowing where to take refuge, pass the night in stairs or any quiet corner they can light upon. Not unfrequently they find their way to the Children's Shelter in the High Street, where they are taken care of by the officials of the Society for the Prevention of Cruelty to Children, or they are picked up in their wanderings by an officer of the Society and made comfortable till their case—and, let us hope, that of their parents also—is disposed of by the Sheriff.

Well may one stand aghast at the barbarity revealed by the records of the cases dealt with by this Society. Here are a few specimen cases out of the hundreds unearthed in the course of a year.

EXCESSIVE BEATING.—Three children, nine, seven, and five, were found in a dark and filthy back room, beyond hearing and far away from neighbours. No food. The father slept on the bed with blankets, the children on the floor. He went out at six, returned at nine. If the children overslept themselves he used to beat them. When brought to the Shelter, the eldest girl had a bad black eye, and her body was severely marked. Father sent to prison for twenty-one days.

ASSAULT.—Infant, aged six months. The mother drunk. The baby was ill, had measles, and large sore on left arm from vaccination. The mother wilfully threw her sick child from her arms twice on to a stone floor. At night, 9 P.M., she was found drunk on the floor of her house, the baby crying and lying on the hearthstone on her sore arm. Mother sent to prison for fourteen days.

ASSAULT.—A girl, aged eight. The mother is a drunkard and a terror to her husband and seven children. For not going to school, the mother took the poker and struck the girl on the eye, the arm and about her body. The doctor said the tissues of her arm felt like a pulp under his touch. Her face was terribly disfigured and swollen. The girl was taken to the Shelter and then sent to an industrial school. The mother was sent to prison for thirty days.

CRUEL NEGLECT.—Five children, ages eleven, eight, seven, five, four, were found all nearly naked, the youngest quite naked, suffering from sores and weak eyes through want. All covered with vermin, no food, no furniture. They had not tasted food from the morning previous to being found. The smell was sickening. The mother sold fish, and left early in the morning, and gave to the children what she could; the father a drunkard, and so heartless that he took the scant clothing off the boy aged four and sold it at a rag shop to get drink. The children taken to Shelter. Father sent to prison for fourteen days.

CRUEL NEGLECT.—Four children, ages twelve, ten, eight, five, were found in an area, living in a cellar, so dark that at twelve noon a light had to be struck before the officer could see the children. They were left in the morning by the mother without food. She would not return until night, usually drunk. They had had no fire for weeks, and were ill and had sores from want and neglect. They were covered with vermin, and the only bed they had was bits of paper picked off the streets. They were taken to the Shelter. Mother sent to prison for one month.

STARVATION.—Four children, ages twelve, ten, eight, five. Mother the widow of a sea captain. She took a large rented house to keep lodgers, but lost her health and was found ill in bed with not a mouthful of food in the house. For days they had had no fire in the cold weather. They were all supplied with food at once and the three youngest were taken to the Shelter.

SELLING VESTAS.—A boy aged ten, his only clothing a torn jacket and a pair of knicker-bockers, in a very dirty state. When asked what his father did, "I never had a father, sir." His mother, found in an attic in Greenside, with three other children; no food, no furniture—not even a little straw. The boy was taken to the Shelter, the mother and children sent to the poorhouse. The boy has since been sent to an industrial school.

SELLING VESTAS.—A girl, aged eleven. This girl was found in Princes Street. Inquiries were made and it was found that there are eight children. Four sell newspapers after school and make 32s. per week. The father drinks and seldom works. He was cautioned,

BEGGING.—Boy, aged ten, found nearly naked begging at west end Princes Street. His father used to wait for him at Tron Church till 2 A.M., and take the money from him. Boy sent to an industrial school, father and mother convicted and admonished.

This thought persists in coming uppermost in one's mind as he looks upon the array of pale and sunken young faces, and listens to their tale of woe, and reads those records of barbarism : let us good British folks put our own house in order before we try to mend the morals of other people ; and when, in a hundred years or so, we have made a favourable impression upon our home-bred savages, it will be time enough to turn our attention to the reformation of the mild mannered barbarians abroad ; otherwise we may yet learn, experimentally, that

> The child's sob in the silence curses deeper
> Than the strong man in his wrath.

IV.

"FURNISHED LODGINGS" IN THE SLUMS.

In the preceding articles we have endeavoured to describe life as it is to be seen in the homes of the very poorest and most degraded denizens of the slums of our city. To some—those to whom the putrid squalor that seethes beneath their feet is nothing but a name—these pictures may have seemed exaggerations, too horrible to be real; we have been told as much. But those who are familiar with the dark places of Edinburgh will unhesitatingly confess that the reality surpasses in hideousness anything that the imagination could create. There are things one sees that defy description, that cannot be written. But they burn themselves into the brain; they can never be forgotten; they come into the mind unbidden in times of warm, well-fed comfort and content—phantasms that chase away cheerful theories of the welfare of future generations.

The one-roomed dwellings we have hitherto explored, filthy holes though they be, are still of the nature of private houses; they and the bits of furniture they hold are, for the time at least, the property of the occupants. The unhappy beings who live in them have not sunk so low but that they retain a desire to have a home of their own.

We now take a step lower in the social scale, and come upon a section of a vast floating population who have never been able to struggle into the position of being masters of their homes, or have never had a wish to be so; or, having once been in that position, have fallen from it through misfortune or their own evil habits. We refer to the occupants of " furnished lodgings " in the slums. These may be said to fill a social position midway between the class who live in private houses and the more deeply sunken multitude who pass their days in common lodging-houses.

Scattered throughout the poorest quarters of the town, sometimes in small groups, at others the whole or portion of a tenement, are hundreds of tiny chambers let out in this manner at exorbitant rents. The rooms are usually like those we have already described, small, dilapidated, and dirty to a degree which people of the better class can scarcely conceive of. To the mind of a housewife in what is called respectable society, a very dirty room is one that has been neglected for

perhaps a day or two. Let such persons of
average tidy habits, however, think of a room,
originally of wretched, dingy appearance, inhabited
by two, three, or half-a-dozen tattered men,
women, and children, whose notions of cleanliness
are not much higher than those of savages, and
who for weeks, or even months, seldom make a
pretence of washing their abode, but allow all
kinds of refuse to accumulate and rot undisturbed;
and then some conception will be formed of the
foulness that prevails in the dwellings of the
poor.

In going in and about those furnished lodgings
we have often thought that they must be exceedingly profitable investments for the proprietors.
The weekly rent generally ranges from four
shillings to four shillings and sixpence, for which
the tenant has a hovel of the kind that usually lets
unfurnished for eighteenpence or two shillings, and
furniture consisting of an aged bedstead, the very
shortest possible allowance of bedclothes, a small
deal table, a rough wooden stool, and, in some
cases, a battered tin kettle and a piece or two of
delf ware. These odds and ends, that might be
bought right off for a few shillings, constitute the
"furniture," for the loan of which the liberal-
minded landlord charges about half-a-crown a

FURNISHED LODGINGS.

week. That is to say, the unhappy tenant pays in the course of a month as much for the hire of the furniture as the furniture itself is worth at a generous estimate. Certainly a very fair return for one's money.

If one believed all the stories one hears about the rapacity of proprietors, he would set the slum land-lord down as a past-master in the art of extortion. Doubtless some of them are. They treat the wretches whom they have in their power as if they had no rights and no feelings, as if they were only so much material made for squeezing pence out of. Every mean dodge that a base ingenuity can invent is resorted to for the purpose of multiplying " extras." Their victims may protest, but complaints and protests are of no avail. The tenant is pretty plainly told that if he is not pleased with the conditions he must bundle and go ; and it may be, if this last advice is adopted, he finds that he has jumped from the frying-pan into the fire.

It was reasons of this kind that caused a young man and his wife, living in the Canongate, to remain in a house—not furnished lodgings—which was in such a disgraceful state that a merciful man would not have stabled his horse in it. The room was a small, smoky den, with a wall on one

side, on which there was no plaster, only a coat or
two of yellow ochre covering the rough hewn
stones. In the corner of the bed recess appeared
half of a doorway that had been built up, and in
the roof above was a great hole about two feet
long by a foot broad. The wall at the foot of the
bed was wet, of a dark brown colour, and gave off
a sickening smell When we asked him the cause
of this state of affairs he told us that the hole had
been made by leakage of water from a closet in
the landing above. Sometimes the overflow was
so great that the water poured through the hole,
down the wall, formed a stream on the floor, and
escaping under the door, ran down the stairs outside. He had had bad health ever since he came
to the house, and at length he had removed the
bed from the recess to the middle of the floor; but
as that placed it between two opposite windows
neither rain nor wind proof, the alteration was
not much of an improvement. The room was a
terribly cold and draughty one. But had he not
asked the landlord to put the closet to rights and
repair the windows? Yes, several times; but he
had been told in effect that if he did not like the
house he was at liberty to remove to another.
And so the hope that the house would some day
be put in proper order and the disinclination to

remove had combined to keep him in that disease-breeding hovel. Besides, he did not know to whom to make representations regarding the insanitary condition of the house. They are ignorant, very ignorant, these poor people, and fall an easy prey to the cheat and the extortioner.

On the other hand, they are uncommonly "contrary" folks to deal with. A landlord may at first regulate his dealings with them by the most elevated, philanthropic principles; but very soon he finds that business cannot be successfully conducted on the lines of pure philanthropy. If he cleans and repairs his houses, they are soon as foul as before, and he discovers to his grief that his tenants use the soil-pipes as rubbish bins, and have a rooted conviction that the wood-work of the rooms is intended to be broken up for firewood in times of emergency. He may try to teach them more civilised habits; he may expostulate or endeavour to shame them into cleanliness. But all his attempts are almost altogether fruitless. Dirty and careless these people are, and they will remain so to the end. It is little cause for wonder, then, that with such incorrigibles to deal with, the landlord relinquishes all thought of reformation, and adopts a purely business basis of procedure. Still we might point to instances where efforts of that kind have been rewarded by most gratifying results, shown in the tidiness of the houses and the mode of life of the inhabitants. The public would receive with a murmur of pleased surprise what might be told of the patient disinterestedness of some men and women in Edinburgh who have property in the slums.

But to return to our furnished lodgings.

The people who conduct their housekeeping on this plan are an exceedingly interesting class of the community, comprising as they do many of those strangely-living, itinerant beings who pick up their livelihood on the streets, and who have not had opportunity or inclination to establish a permanent household—such as beggars and street musicians. Thieves likewise find this a convenient mode of domestic life, for they have the quiet of a private house, which cannot be got in a common lodging-house, without any encumbrances that might be awkward in the event of hurried removal being considered advisable. Furnished lodgings are suitable also for couples who marry very young or are improvident. Such persons can start matrimonial life without the initial expense of furnishing a house; but this is a bad beginning to make, for once they become accustomed to lodgings the probability is that they will continue in them, and never get the length of having a fixed abode—a state of affairs not at all conducive to family comfort or stability.

One instance will suffice to illustrate the habits of those nomadic tribes.   In a dreary little room in the West Port we had a talk with the lodger, a young pavement artist of somewhat prepossessing appearance.   The room—it goes without saying that it was horribly dirty—contained a bed, a small table, a backless chair, and an upturned box ; while a candle, stuck against the wall, shed a sickly light around, and, at the same time, decorated the walls with long streaks of smoke and soot.   Upon the upturned box the artist's wife, a mere girl, sat with her head in her hands, a picture of shabby, dishevelled dejection ; the artistic young man himself, just returned from an unremunerative day's work on the pavement, was making a tasteless supper of a chunk of bread. He had had "hard lines" all that week.   That day (Thursday) was the first that week favourable to his calling, and though he had stood at his pictures all the day, he had earned only twopence. But such poor drawings were the exception, not the rule.   In summer days (people will not stand

D

to look at pictures in winter when the frost is nipping their toes and making their noses blue) he makes a comfortable living; and that is just where the mischief comes in. So long as those fellows can get along without doing any steady work, they will do so; though one would imagine that loafing is about as laborious an occupation as any one could be employed in. The street artist, however, loafs to some purpose. He told us that on New Year's Day he took up his position on the Lothian Road, and in the course of the forenoon, until a policeman commanded him to "move on," he made twelve shillings. The largest sum he ever made in one day was at Perth races, when his day's earnings amounted to thirty shillings. But, as he said, his sort of life was only "a hunger and a burst;" at one time he would be in clover, and then a spell of bad weather would reduce him almost to starvation. He was glad in these circumstances to do any odd job that could keep him alive till the tide turned.

This is a fair specimen of the thriftless, shiftless persons who never get beyond the unhomelike furnished lodgings.

As we have already said, thieves are generally supposed to favour this style of domestic economy.

One of the rooms we visited—"by special per-
mission," so to speak—was inhabited by a gang
of housebreakers and pickpockets. Their apartment was quite a model one of its kind; it was
not so hopelessly filthy, but it contained nothing
more than the usual stools, table, and bed. In
consideration of a bed-closet being attached to
the room the rent was six shillings a week, and
this the light-fingered gang—three hangdog-look-
ing men with eight-piece caps and spotted neck-
cloths, and a brawny woman with a hoarse voice
—paid amongst them. They worked together,
each having a special department of business to
attend to. A middle-aged man, who appeared
to be the captain of the crew, did housebreaking
and other jobs of importance. A quiet young
man did the prospecting; that is, he looked
about him for likely "cribs" for his pals to
"crack," with a view to which he would clean
windows and do other similar light work that
procures for the operator entrance into houses
and shops. The muscular female also had her
duties strictly defined, the principal one being
to act as "decoy" when her male copartners
had pocket-picking business on hand.

With many poor families life too often resolves
itself into nothing but a desperate struggle to

meet the weekly payment of four shillings for lodgings. The father, it may be, loses his health, and the mother has to take up the labour of the bread-winner. She goes out hawking or charing, or engages in the loathsome work of "bucket-ranging;" frequently she is reduced almost entirely to this last employment. Scarcely anything can be made out of it now-a-days, paper is so cheap, and people seem to be more careful of what goes into the refuse-box. So old cinder-gatherers have told us. A woman, with a husband and a family depending upon her, will rise up in the early morning and make a raid on the ash-buckets, and perhaps twopence or threepence will be the total result of her industry. Cinders she carefully preserves for use at home; while pieces of bread and meat are eagerly rescued from the dust-heap, and go to replenish the exhausted family larder. In this way they keep life in, and every available halfpenny of money is husbanded for the purpose of keeping a roof above their heads. But even with this constant pinching the rent frequently cannot be gathered, for four shillings is a considerable sum to those poor creatures. In that eventuality their fate depends very much on the character of the landlord. If he is an individual of average tender-heartedness, they are usually allowed a period of grace; but eviction generally quickly ensues. One landlady has a practice of removing the bedclothes, so as to precipitate the removal of her non-rent-paying tenants.

Thus thrust out into the streets, those unlucky wretches subsist as best they can till a return of prosperity enables them to take to furnished lodgings again, only, however, to tread the same weary round of adversity, where change is but a variation in the degree of suffering.

V.

COMMON LODGING-HOUSES.

WE come now to a lower circle in this Inferno—the third. We have had glimpses of life as it is to be seen in the one-roomed dwelling of the poor man; we have also looked at the conditions of existence a grade further down, where the system of "furnished lodgings" is in vogue; our next descent is to the sphere of the common lodging-house. The people who live in common lodging-houses may be said to be in the very lowest strata of our population, embracing as they do inferior artisans and labourers, criminals of all kinds, tramps and beggars; all those pitiable beings, in fact, who because of misfortune or bad character, have never been able to gain an independent position in life, but drift about, like straws in the gutter, a misery to themselves and a constant annoyance and burden to the community.

Lodging-houses, of course, differ in degrees of respectability. One house may be noted for its cleanliness, orderliness, and general good manage-

ROOM FOR TWO FAMILIES IN A LODGING-HOUSE.

ment. Another may have a bad reputation as a refuge for thieves, and women of questionable character, and, accordingly, have the eye of the police continually upon it. A third may be the favourite "howff" of the tramp tribe; while resident mendicants make a fourth their customary "doss-house."

Like their reputations, the internal arrangements of common lodging-houses are after a variety of patterns. In general, however, they are planned in this simple and comprehensive style. From the street a passage, in which there is a pay-box like a railway booking-office, leads to the general kitchen, where the lodgers cook and eat their food, and lounge, talk, and smoke. Upstairs, as many flats as you please, are the bed-rooms and dormitories with the accommodation painted in large letters on the doors. These rooms may be bedded for any number of people, from two up to forty, or even more. Some of them are wonderfully clean — considering the habits of their occupants: some of them are no tidier than they should be; and not a few are execrably dirty.

But what will strike one as the most notable feature of the sleeping-rooms in common lodging-houses is the scant attention paid to privacy in the married quarters.   One would expect that in houses licensed by our Magistrates and under their direct supervision, the bed-rooms would be arranged with more regard to the dictates of decency than is found in a Zulu kraal or a Patagonian mud-hut.   And this disregard is only emphasised by a pretence made to preserve the "sacred secrecy" of the family.   It is quite a common thing to see one room occupied by two or three married couples and their children. The beds are placed end to end, and are separated only by a board the width of the bed and about the height of a man.   This partition is a mere make-believe, a nominal concession to propriety, and does not afford the slightest seclusion to any of the occupants of the room.   The obvious pretentiousness of the arrangement irritates one.   The erection of the screen is a tacit admission that there ought to be seclusion, but one might as well attempt to secure it by sticking a twopenny Japanese fan between the beds as by putting up these boards.

The lodgers themselves do not seem to deprecate this publicity; they move about among each other without restraint or bashfulness, each family acting as if there were no strange eyes looking upon them.   Such is the effect of habit.

THE KITCHEN OF A GRASSMARKET LODGING-HOUSE.

"A lodging-house is no place for a man who has a wife and bairns. Some of them are perfect hells, and none of them are heavens," said a man to us who had had a long and varied experience of life in these houses. Doubtless this would be the opinion of most people of similar experience; yet their efforts to escape from their baneful surroundings are seldom attended with success. The attempt is often made. A man and his wife will leave a lodging-house they have lived in for some time, saying that they intend to set up a home of their own. But the chances are that in a few weeks, or months at the most, they are back again in their old quarters, driven there by their old enemy, drink. "There are very few of them need be here at all, if it were not for drink; if it was not for that, they would have houses of their own," a Grassmarket lodging-house keeper remarked to us. "They can never gather enough money to enable them to begin housekeeping; but if they do, they soon break out again, drink up everything, and come back again worse off than ever. Once they become accustomed to the lodging-house life they seldom get out of it."

The kitchen of a lodging-house is an exceedingly interesting place. There the picturesque may be studied under conditions not easily found else-

where.   One kitchen we have in our mind's eye is
representative of most of them.   It was a long,
low-roofed room, with a stone floor.   At one end
there was a big, old-fashioned fireplace, in which
a mighty fire roared and crackled.   On a stool at
a corner of the hearth sat a ragged old man toast-
ing a red herring of powerful odour spitted upon
a stick.   In front of the fire, assiduously stirring
the contents of a hanging pot, stood a nut-cracker
faced old woman, so bent, so wrinkled, and
altogether so " uncanny " looking, that one would
have thought it quite in keeping with her appearance if she had suddenly vanished up the chimney
astride a broomstick.   On benches on either side
of the room and around the fire sat a score or
more of the seediest, motliest beings that one
could well gather together.   Women in short
kirtles, with their bare arms folded or set akimbo,
were " chaffing " men with dirty unshaven faces,
battered hats, and garments that an old-clothes-
man would have nothing to say to.   Some of those
dingy lodgers, men and women alike, were smoking ; some lay asleep on benches, and some sat
gazing dreamily into space.   Several unwashed
children were disporting themselves with a bandy-
legged mongrel dog, which seemed to be the
joint possession of the whole colony.   In a corner

a man of dilapidated exterior was cutting the hair of one of his "pals," an operation which drew forth facetious remarks from several of the onlookers, their humour finding vent in speculating as to where he got the previous "crop" and where he was likely to get the next one.

It was a Sunday, and though it was past four o'clock in the afternoon most of the men had just risen, and were dressing by easy stages. Quite a number of the lodgers of the house, in fact, did not leave their beds at all; for not being addicted to the habit of church-going, and finding the Sunday .quietude of the Grassmarket irksome, they preferred to pass the day in slumber. Besides, as not unfrequently happens, when a man has not got anything in the larder, he finds it easier to stifle the complainings of an empty stomach in bed than in loafing about the streets or sniffing viands cooking in the kitchen.

In a lodging-house each one does his own cooking, unless a number of persons agree to co-operate to save trouble. Every one for himself, however, is the general rule. But, then, this sort of people don't go in for elaborate culinary effects. A bit of bacon fried, a roasted herring, and such easily-cooked morsels, with a piece of bread, cheese, and tea, form their staple bill-of-fare.

Each lodger has a small locker, in which he stows away any property or provisions he may be possessed of; but, as one man ruefully observed, "they're no' o' much use, for it's no' often that we've mair than the smell to lock awa'."

The charge usually made in common lodging-houses is 6d. a day for each individual; if a person stays a whole week he pays only for six days, the seventh day's lodging being given free of charge. When, say, two or three families occupy a room such as the one shown in the sketch, they each pay 4s. a week, making 8s. or 12s. a week that the proprietor draws for the rent of one room of insignificant size and wretched furnishings, which consist of the beds, a table, and a bench or two.

In the Model Lodging-house in the Grass-market the rates are 4d, 5d., and 6d., without a free day on Sunday. Its internal arrangements are as much superior to those of the average lodging-house as a well-regulated hotel surpasses a low cook-shop. The building is large and airy, as clean as a man-of-war; the bunks are neat and comfortable, the dormitories admirably ventilated; and in addition to a large dining hall and a cooking range, there is a well-appointed reading room.

"Why don't you prefer to go to the Model Lodging-house?" we asked a dirty specimen of the tramp tribe whom we met in one of the least washed "doss-houses" in the city. "Well, ye see, sir," he replied, "we havena got the freedom there that we have here. There are ower mony rules and regulations in the Model. Ye're no allowed to lie in your bed a' day if ye want to, or to gang aboot as ye like. There are ower mony men in uniform goin' aboot for my taste." In the estimation of this man, and of his kind, the lousy freedom of the den he kennelled in was more to be desired than the cleanliness and regularity of the Model Lodging-house.

There really is a Bohemianism about the life in a common lodging that suits the tastes of those restless, careless characters; and in their own way they have jolly carousals now and again.

One Saturday night, as we were climbing the stair to a lodging-house noted as a resort of hawkers, beggars, and street musicians, we heard sounds of uproarious merriment coming from the kitchen. When we entered we were confronted with a grotesque scene. The room was filled with a hilarious company, picturesque in their rags. In the centre of the floor, surrounded by a laughing, joking, applauding group, were a man and a woman going hard at an Irish jig, putting as much agility into their toes and heels as if their reputations depended on their exertions, as no doubt they did. The room was stiflingly hot, and the boots of the man and the woman were by no means of dancing-shoe make, but they kept it up without faltering or flagging for a moment. And right good dancers they were too, not merely shuffling through with any sort of apology for figures, but whirling, linking, and setting, all in perfect time and step. Faster and faster scraped the fiddler, faster and faster twinkled the feet of the dancers, and louder grew the whooping and applauding of the spectators.

At length the man gave in and withdrew, but the woman, whose excited eye and whisky-reeking breath betrayed the secret of her exuberance, vociferously called upon another partner. Again the jigging began, and soon waxed as furious as ever. However, despite the whisky and the boisterous cries of encouragement from the onlookers, the woman's endurance was eventually exhausted, and, panting and perspiring, the dancers sank on to a bench. Then came a singing interlude with violin accompaniment, at the conclusion of which the flagstones again began to resound with the clatter of swiftly moving feet.

A SATURDAY NIGHT REVEL IN A LOD

That night with the jolly beggars was a glimpse of the bright side of lodging-house life, a brief lifting of the heavy clouds that overshadow existence there. The normal conditions, however, are painfully sombre; they are poverty and hunger, filth, wretchedness and wickedness, degradation and despair.

VI.

TRAMPS AND THEIR WAYS.

WE have arrived now at the fourth stage in our descent in the social scale, passing the poor man as he·is found at home, in furnished lodgings, and in common lodging-houses, till we come to the habitual rover, who calls no place his home, who belongs to no particular town, county, or country, but is for ever on the move ; wandering, he cares not whither and knows not why.

Adopting a famous phraseology, it may be said that some are born tramps, some drift into tramp-life, and some have tramp-life thrust upon them. The first-mentioned class are those who have been born " on the road," the children of tramps, reared in the profession, and remaining in it all their lives. There is such a thing as hereditary tramphood ; the tendency to rove seems to run in the blood like physical or mental traits ; with this difference, that the wandering propensity does not jump one generation and reappear in the next, as inherited idiosyncracies commonly do.

We know of at least one noted tramp, whose father and grandfather were tramps before him, and who, at the present moment, is bringing up a large and promising family to his ancestral vocation.

Those who have tramp-life thrust upon them are not, we believe, a large section of the brotherhood, for the act of entering the calling is almost always more or less voluntary. Yet it frequently happens that a man may be dragged into the life against his will.

For example, a man living with his wife and family in Edinburgh, finds himself suddenly thrown out of employment. Unable to obtain work here, he sets off for Glasgow on foot. There he finds something to do, in a few weeks sends for his family, and they, selling off their modest furniture, join the bread-winner in Glasgow. But soon he is again without work, and this time he migrates to Dundee, perhaps, whither the family follow him at the earliest possible day. A few moves of this kind soon begin to tell upon the habits of a household. The mother and the children, left behind while the father is looking for work in another city, become initiated into the mysteries of the begging business; domestic stability rapidly goes; and in the course of time the family are enlisted in the ragged regiment that are constantly parading every highway in the country.   Once they adopt that career they very, very seldom forsake it.   Life then is but a slouch onward to the poor house, or until they lie down to die behind a hedge.

But the genuine, thoroughbred tramp—he who may be said to have of his own will adopted the profession—is a shiftless, lazy rascal whose chief aim is to get through life with the least possible amount of labour.   His aversion to work might be said to amount almost to a passion, were it not that he is too easy-going to harbour such a strong feeling.   His disinclination to exertion takes rather the form of a placid determination not to be moved from the passive attitude he has assumed with respect to the industrial system. To this line of conduct he adheres with a persistency quite pathetic in its steadfastness.

There is a story told of two tramps that deserves to be true if it is not.   They had fallen asleep in a cosy corner in an out-house and were snoring as loudly as if they had earned their repose, when one of them began to stir uneasily and to give vent to half-stifled moans.   These symptoms of dispeace increased until he awoke with a shriek, and trembling violently.   "What's the matter?" anxiously inquired his companion who had been roused by the commotion. "Oh, something awful," groaned the man with the nightmare, as he buried his face in his hands. "I've had a terrible dream. *I dreamt I was working!*" Only a tramp could appreciate the horror of a vision like that.

Circumstances, however, are sometimes more than a match for the tramp, so that he finds himself reduced to the absolute necessity of throwing off his coat and expending some of his precious energy. And this leads us to note that, broadly speaking, tramps may be classified for the sake of convenience into "working" and "non-working."

The "working" tramp is a man (or woman) who wanders about the country "in search of work," as he puts it when making his piteous appeal to charitable persons and societies. He works for a day or two or a week or two in a town, then off he goes to some other place. The demon of unrest seems to possess him. He cannot remain long in one place; he has not sufficient fixity of purpose for that. "Give a tramp the best job in Scotland, and, ten to one, he won't stop at it," said a man to us who had himself been in the profession, but had had the rare good fortune to be weaned from it. You may get him to work steadily for a little while, but just as you are beginning to believe in his reformation, he becomes restless and dissatisfied, drinks any savings he may have made, and breaks loose once more.

One of the worst instances we have known of temporary reform followed by complete relapse was that of a tramp who, coming under powerful influence, settled down to sobriety and the business of a fish hawker. Being a smart fellow, he prospered, and in the course of three years bought a horse and cart, and saved £133. But one unfortunate night he broke his pledge, and "got on the spin." It seemed as if a devil had taken possession of him. Nothing could stop his mad career. In ten months he drank the £133 he had in the bank, and his horse and cart, in addition to the money he earned in sober intervals during that time. Thus reduced to his former poverty he took to the road again, and is a more confirmed tramp than before. As well try to harpoon the wind as attempt to fix these rovers to any permanent employment.

These tramps of intermittent industry are to be met with in great numbers on the roads leading to large commercial centres. From Glasgow to Dundee is their favourite route, thence through the small but busy manufacturing towns of Fife to Edinburgh, from which they slowly make their way back again to Glasgow. Many spend almost their entire lives on this tour, tramping and working, and working and tramping, doing the round over and over again, with an occasional excursion, perhaps, to Newcastle or Carlisle, or some other distant part. But wherever they go, it is with the same aimlessness, and productive of as little abiding benefit.

Even a more hopeless subject to deal with is the "non-working" tramp, who resembles his spasmodic relation in everything except that he is *not* "in search of work." On the contrary, if he had the faintest suspicion that work was in search of *him* he would run till he dropped to escape from it. People of this class are simply itinerant beggars who rove at large over the country, wandering wherever they think they are likely to get the most with the least trouble. Many of them have not done a day's work for years, but by begging, singing, or playing a whistle in the streets of the towns and villages they pass through, they contrive to make a tolerable livelihood. These mendicants do not confine their tramping to the highways connecting commercial towns, as their "working" brethren do, but ramble all over the country, scouring agricultural as well as manufacturing districts. Indeed, it is said that they fare better among country folks than with the sharper town-bred people.

A tattered and battered fellow whom we got into conversation with some time ago, belonged to this class of tramps. He was one of those cool, brazen-faced individuals who could stare a sheriff-officer out of countenance; one of those calm, self-satisfied persons who are never disconcerted and never in a hurry.

"I have been a fortnight in Edinburgh," he said. "Have been in it often before. It is a capital place for resting my feet, and I generally stay in it a fortnight at a time, for there are any amount of 'skippers' [places for passing the night in] all round about. I get as good a living as if I was working. By a little mouching I can get as much grub as I need, and I can rest myself whenever I like. But a man would be better off if he could fiddle or whistle or do anything of that kind. I made the price of my 'doss' [bed] with a tin whistle yesterday on the High Street and Bank Street; made sixpence in ten minutes, and that got doss, tea, and sugar. I do work occasionally to give myself a fresh start. I have been in two or three regiments and deserted. In the

winter, when I was hard up, I gave myself up, but
soon deserted again, and set off on the road in
a fresh rig. I was a militiaman for four years, and
that kept me from settling down, having to leave
my work every year to go up for training. I have
been on tour for two years; during winter get into skippers; in summer-time travel through the
night and sleep anywhere during the day, under
a hedge or on the roadside, only occasionally
getting a bed by singing 'The Highlandman's
Toast,' and 'Flora Macdonald's Lament.' I have
got many a copper by singing them during the
past six years. I learned them from a song-book.
I am quite happy and contented with my lot. I
could do like other folk, but don't care to
work."

Another happy-go-lucky bird of passage, during
one of his periodical visits to "this paradise of
tramps," as Edinburgh has been called, explained
his mode of travel to us; and his account we
shall reproduce, omitting, of course, the tramp
jargon, which would be unintelligible to most
people.

"Say, now, that I left Glasgow, bound for
Dundee. Well, the first day I would try to get
as far as Stirling, for there is a good night-shelter
there. The next day would be an easy one, only

a six mile walk to Dunblane, where there is a kind inspector of poor who often gives us the price of our lodging. The next night would see me at Auchterarder, where I would find a sleeping-place of some kind; and on the fourth day I would reach Perth. Though that is a good-sized town, it has not got a shelter, but there are lots of cosy dosses to be got in the farmhouses round about. The fifth night I would sleep at Errol, where I would probably get my bed from the inspector of the poor; and on the sixth day I would reach Dundee. There, of course, I would put up at the night-shelter. The next morning I would perhaps look for work, or sing in the streets, or beg, and if I got any money, pass the night in a lodging-house. But if I got no money, I would sleep in the most comfortable corner I could find."

This is a specimen tour; all tramps' excursions are managed on the same general principles.

When a tramp shuffles into Edinburgh, from whatever point of the compass he comes, he usually makes his way at night to the Night Asylum in Old Fishmarket Close, adjoining the Police Office. There he takes his place among a waiting crew of poor wretches, who, like himself, are without place to lay their head.

About eight o'clock the applicants for a night's

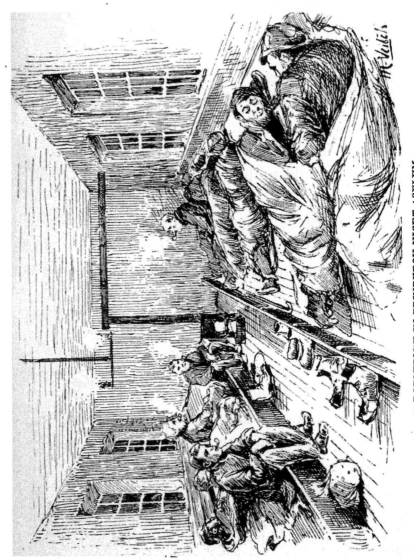

A DORMITORY IN EDINBURGH NIGHT ASYLUM.

shelter are gathered together in the hall of the asylum, and one by one, are brought before the superintendent, who asks them their name, age, occupation, when and where they last worked and where they are going, and some other personal details. The rule of the establishment is that none but strangers are admitted, and not more than once in three months. The superintendent, however, has power to relax the regulations in special cases, and frequently considerable pains are taken to give assistance to persons of whose good character assurances have been obtained. It is impossible in the nature of things to guard against imposition altogether; consequently, it is to be feared that many lazy, skulking fellows get better treatment than they deserve.

Be that as it may, when all the applicants have passed through the catechism, and got back to their seats in the hall, where they sit a silent, dirty, ragged company, a supper of porridge and milk is handed round in tin basins. For a few minutes nothing is heard but the scraping of the spoons on the bowls as the hungry outcasts put themselves outside the porridge with amazing rapidity. Then they all flock upstairs to the dormitories. These are not sumptuous apartments, but they are warm, comfortable, and

scrupulously clean. Down both sides of a long
room sloping platforms are raised about a foot
from the floor, and on these, wrapped in a rug,
the homeless creatures sleep. A stove in the
middle of the room keeps the temperature agree
able. Smoking is forbidden, but it is difficult
prevent men having a whiff during the night, an
possibly, the tobacco fumes may act as a dis
fectant, which, it need scarcely be said, is
powerful argument in favour of permitting t'
practice. In the morning the lodgers get brea
fast, and are then allowed to shift for themselve

Our friend the tramp will probably "mouch
about the city during the day, and if when nigh
draws near, he has not enough money to get a
bed in a lodging-house, he will trudge down to
Leith and creep on board a coal-boat, or a tug,
or he will leave the town and make for the nearest pithead, brickwork, coke-ovens, farmhouse,
or, in fact, any place where he can find a warm
shelter. He delights to coil himself up in a
boiler-house or beside a glowing ash-heap. Not
unfrequently, poor fellow, he pays for this comfort
with his life, for while he sleeps he is suffocated
by poisonous fumes, and in the morning his
charred body is found lying on the cinders.

It is a curious fact that tramps seldom pass the

night in stairs and such-like retreats of the destitute in towns.   It is usually street loafers and
resident beggars who do that.   The true tramp
prefers the open country.

A tramp's knowledge of the country through
which his beat lies is as peculiar as it is varied.
He knows the farms where a shakedown of straw
in an outhouse may be counted upon ; he remem-
bers also the steadings whose owners discounte-
nance his visits and where the watch-dogs are
corruptible.   Towns and villages are mapped
out according to their relative hospitality.   If he
in a communicative mood he will tell you that
Dalkeith is one of the "hungriest holes in all
Scotland" for tramps, and that he would give
the palm for parsimony to the village of Cock-
burnspath.   On the other hand the place where
tramps receive the most generous treatment is,
he thinks, in the fishing village of Eyemouth : the
reason why, he does not know, except that
it is because fisher-folks are simple-minded,
kindly people.

With such knowledge as this at his finger-ends,
a gentleman of the road can lead not an unpleas-
ant life in summer-time.   In winter, however, he
has to put up with many hardships.   But if he is
a man of resource, he can usually hit upon some

plan to secure his comfort during the cold months. He may retire gracefully to the poor-house or the hospital and lie there snug until the return of weather favourable to travelling. To make themselves eligible for residence in the infirmary, tramps. resort to all sorts of tricks. They have been known to run a knife into their hand or to disable themselves in some other wa One man we were told of could simulate pal so well as to defy detection by the doctors, an another could so contort his face as to make th. medical men believe that he was in a very bac way indeed.

Another aimiable weakness that tramps have is that of passing themselves off as unemployed during strikes or in times of commercial distress. Whenever a strike occurs in any district thither the tramps flock, and for the nonce take up the profession of the unemployed, and a very easy and paying job it is too.

There are some tramps who save money. One we know of is roving about at this present moment with £90 sewed in the lining of his coat. Another, the last time he left Edinburgh, carried with him a bank book showing a credit balance of over £100. But these are rare excep-tions. The ordinary tramp lives from day to day, from hand to mouth, at the expense of the public; and when at length he has trudged his last mile, and lays himself down to die in the poorhouse hospital, he makes his last exaction upon society for the amount of his funeral expenses.

VII.

THE HOMELESS.

It was a bitterly cold Saturday night in March. The east wind was whistling down the deserted streets, making the chimney pots creak and sway, and the lamp-lights hiss and flicker. The only policeman on the street had stepped aside for a moment into an archway to take refuge from a more than usually angry blast that came shrieking along the causeway. Bending our bodies as we faced the onrush, we pulled our mufflers further over our chins, and thrust our hands deep into our pockets.

A night piercingly cold indeed, that caused us to shrink and shiver, and think of blazing fires and cosy beds, though we had but newly risen from specially substantial supper, and were heavily coated.

One o'clock boomed sullenly from a church steeple as we passed under the shadow of the building, and warned us to quicken our steps in the direction our business of exploration led us.

OUTCAST—ONE O'CLOCK IN THE MORNING.

"For the love o' God gie me a fill o' baccy," said a hoarse, harsh voice, as we turned the corner of the church; and, stepping aside, we saw a woman sitting in a corner of a doorway. The person who had thus addressed us was a thinly-clothed woman of barely middle-age. Her face was thin and bruised, and bore traces of recent bleeding; she was without hat or jacket; her thread-bare close-fitting dress showed a bony, meagre figure. With one arm she held a sleeping boy to her breast, and with her disengaged hand carefully shielded from the wind a short clay pipe, which she was smoking with eagerness.

"Just one fill," she repeated, in a pleading tone, as we approached her. The excessive solicitude of her manner aroused our curiosity, and as the business that had brought us out that night was the search for such homeless ones as she, we opened a conversation with her. She said she had led a wandering life since she had been deserted by the father of her child. By begging and an occasional spell of work she sometimes earned enough to pay for a bed in a common lodging-house, but it was by no means a rare thing for her to pass the night in all weathers, sleeping in stairs, passages, or cellars. When we came up she was turning over in her mind the various places where she could huddle up for the night. As she spoke, she smoked with intense relish ; her pipe seemed to be a luxury that she laid extraordinary value upon. Poor wretch ! it was her only solace, and her thanks were profuse when we gave her enough tobacco to serve for several "fills."

"Would she go to a lodging-house if we paid for her?" we asked. The alacrity with which she rose when this proposal was made was sufficient answer; so we made our way to the nearest lodging. At the first place we came to we had the door slammed in our faces; the strong-lunged female who answered to our rapping would not let "that woman" in, for reasons which she did not vouchsafe to us. No amount of argument from us, delivered through the keyhole, could move the porteress one whit from her resolution, and we were compelled to conduct the shivering outcast to another lodging-house. This had a reputation as frightful as its interior was filthy and gloomy, but at such a late hour we could not pick and choose, and, in truth, our companion gave un-mistakable indications that wherever she put up for the night the company would not be worse than herself.

While we were arranging for two nights'

lodging, we had time to look round the kitchen
and note the appearance of the den and its occupants. It was nothing better than a foul,
tumble-down cellar. On benches at the fire,
though it was now nearing two o'clock in the
morning, three or four men and a young woman
were sitting, talking and smoking, the woman
taking turn about with a dirty "cutty" with a
man who sat with his arm round her waist. In
the middle of the floor a half-intoxicated man was
exchanging obscene jests with an unwholesome
female, whose bunch of keys suspended at the
waist marked her as the housekeeper. It was
a scene that one reads of in stories of low life,
and, ignorantly, pooh-poohs as grossly exagger-
ated.

In this congenial company we left the woman
whom we had picked up in the street, carrying
with us her thanks for having provided her with
a shelter for the night. Certainly we wished we
could have seen her in a better place; but whatever the character of the dwelling, it was a regis-
tered lodging-house.

We have described this case in detail because it
is a typical one. There are scores, probably
hundreds of women in Edinburgh who drag out
an existence in this way; homeless and hopeless,

F

begging and sinning their way through life, ready for nameless deeds of degradation if only they can thereby earn a meal, a dram, or a bed. They beg in the streets by day, and if unsuccessful can do nought but haunt the streets for worse purposes at night; and when midnight is long past, and all chances of earning a dishonest penny are gone, they creep into a stair and sleep fitfully till the return of day, which, alas! brings with it but another round of hunger and shame.

People in comfortable circumstances are, we believe, under the impression that "sleeping out" is almost a thing of the past, or at all events is practised only in such places as the East end of London, reports of whose squalid misery periodically startle the world. This is quite an erroneous impression. We have no means of obtaining exact statistics, but make bold to say that the people in Edinburgh who frequently or habitually pass the night in stairs and other convenient places may be numbered by hundreds.

The Grassmarket and the streets in its neighbourhood seem to be the favourite haunts of those social pariahs. A great many of the stairs in those localities are built of stone two or three flats up, but the steps and passages above that are made of wood, and are thus warmer and more comfortable

A NIGHT IN A COLD CORNER.

for sleeping purposes. It is to those long, dark,
narrow passages that the "dead-broke" slummite
repairs at night. Usually he loafs about the
streets till long after midnight in the hope that
something will turn up, and with the object,
also, of escaping the police, who make their first
round at such obscure retreats about that hour.
If a policeman pounces upon one of those
wretches asleep he routs him out and bids him
"move on;" though to what spot he can move
where he will be secure from disturbance neither
he nor the policeman knows. We have discovered
sleepers-out who have taken up their quarters in
a condemned dwelling—such refuges are eagerly
sought after by that class—and having fastened
the door from the inside, could not be persuaded
to open it again, so convinced were they that we
were their natural enemies, the police, come to
turn them out.

It is not in every large town that polite society
objects to the houseless beggar passing the night
in its passages and stair-foots. We can speak at
least of Dublin, where such a restriction does not
appear to be enforced. At midnight in the Irish
capital any one walking through the principal
thoroughfares will be surprised to see recumbent
figures at the base of the O'Connell statue which

were not visible in the daytime, and at every sheltered corner, where the architectural features of the building afford a convenient recess—notably at the Bank — mysterious, unshapely bundles which, on examination, prove to be houseless vagabonds courting "sweet sleep" under the open sky. But in Edinburgh, as we have shown, it is different; and the homeless must creep away out of reach of the policeman's bull's-eye to pass the night undisturbed.

When exploring the slums one wet and stormy night, we climbed a high tenement in the Cowgate and began to grope and stumble about in the maze of lobbies that honeycomb those crowded dwellings. We had quite lost ourselves in the twistings and turnings of one of the narrow passages, and were striking matches in order more readily to find our way out, when we saw huddled up in a sort of recess off the main passage into which two or three doors opened, what appeared to be one or more figures evidently asleep. A closer examination showed us a man and a woman —the latter having an infant wrapped close to her breast in a ragged and dirty shawl. It was a pitiful sight. The man looked so like death in sleep that we thought at first we had chanced upon a more tragic scene than we anticipated.

His almost fleshless bones, his pale, yellow skin, and his hanging jaw were startling in their counterfeit presentment of death. He had propped himself against the wall, and in this position he partly supported his wife, whose rain-soaked garments made her shiver as she lay asleep.

A slight shake woke the man from his slumbers, and when he had recovered from his surprise, he was easily induced to tell his story. He was a labourer, but for some time back, owing to bad health, he had worked only intermittently. They had gradually sold all their belongings, and for a year past had lived chiefly in lodging-houses when they were able to pay their way. Often, however, they had no money, and were compelled to spend the night outside.

Our conversation soon woke the woman, whose worn face assumed a look of eager inquiry, while her fingers worked nervously to fasten the shawl more closely round her child. It was a marvel that the infant lived. It was thin and shrivelled, and the tiny pinched face told more forcibly than words how it must have shared the privations of its parents. We asked the man if the morrow might chance to brighten his prospects, but he answered in a listless way that he could not tell;

he hoped it would. He put his arm round his
wife, and let her rest her head upon his shoulder,
and became in a moment apparently quite oblivious
of our presence.

Such a woful group they made. They looked
as if death would have been a welcome relief from
their misery, and certainly the world seemed to
have no joys for them. Still it was touching to
see how they clung together in their extremity.
Starving and homeless, with rags for their covering, this miserable pair were not to be separated,
and even in their utter destitution they seemed to
find some solace in each other's company, and in
their mutual affection.

Many children and young people of both sexes
are to be found sleeping out at night. They are
reduced to this extremity by the desertion or cruelty
of their parents. To escape the fury of a drunken
father or mother the bairns will flee from the house,
and, not daring to return till the brute is sober, sleep
wherever they can find a corner to crouch in. A
lad whom we met in the Cowgate about two
o'clock one winter morning, told us that he rarely
slept at home on Saturday nights, for " money
being rough " then, drunkenness was the order of
the day, and his father was like a devil when he
had been " smelling the cork." So he made it a

point to avoid the house every Saturday night, and sleep in a stair or an unoccupied house. If he had time and was not too tired, he would walk out to Corstorphine and sleep in a hay-stack, returning home on Sunday afternoon, by which time the evil spirit would have departed from his father.

Again, when a child does not make enough money at business on the street to satisfy the harpies at home, it fears to face them, and prefers to sleep out in company with others in a like position. Thus they are often met with lying in dark corners huddled together for warmth. We were informed by a woman who lived in one of the tenements much frequented by sleepers-out, that one night when the snow was on the ground, and the weather was bitterly cold, ten boys passed the night in the lobby outside her door. It goes without saying that exposure of this kind accounts for much of the enormous mortality among our slum children; the mystery is how any of the poor little things can suffer such hardships and live. Their survival is a sad illustration of the tenacity of human life.

We once had a curious adventure when on the out-look for homeless children. While exploring the intricacies of a long and narrow alley, we descended a short flight of steps so slippery and uneven that a footing was only obtained with difficulty. It was a dreadful night of rain, and we were in such a sloppy and sodden condition that we almost began to wish we were snugly tucked up in bed; but having started on our expedition, we determined to go through with it.

We were now in a narrow, muddy passage, which seemed half open and half covered. Another flight of steps took us quite into subterranean regions, where, in a passage dark as pitch, several cellar doors were indistinctly visible by a feeble light coming from we knew not whither. Thinking we heard voices, we crept stealthily along to where the passage took a sharp turn, and there discovered the origin of the flickering light.

Through the gaping hinge of a half-open rickety door we saw three ragged lads, about fifteen or sixteen years of age, squatting on the floor and engrossed in a game of cards, which they played by the light of a candle stump. So eager were they in their play they were not aware of our approach, which, of course, had not been altogether unattended by noise, and surprised at the extraordinary sight, we remained in a sense spellbound, watching the progress of the game. From the remarks dropped we could gather that the game was being played for turns at the pipe, the winner receiving the pipe and puffing at it until the next game was decided, when he would either retain it or hand it to one of his companions. But a muttered curse now and again escaping from the lips of the youthful players showed how earnest and deep was their interest.

One of the lads had his face turned full towards us, and the candle being fixed to a stone immediately in front of him, lighted up his features, so that we could scan them carefully. The rain, which had soaked his tattered cap and run down his face in black streams, had not improved his appearance, but such a pair of sharp, bright, eager, roguish eyes, as every second glanced along his cards and flashed a look upon his comrades as they followed up his play, it would be difficult to match. The lads—dirty, ragged, and wet—seemed for the time quite regardless of their miserable plight, for only the direst need could have compelled them to spend such a night in such a hole. They seemed, indeed, to be trying to forget their discomforts in play. A shuffle of the cards gave breathing space for a minute, and the pipe was then passed round, the smoker evidently relinquishing it with as much regret as the other received it with joy. We whispered to each other to enter suddenly and observe the effect, but before any such intention could be carried out, a careless movement warned the little gamesters of our presence. In an instant all was darkness. We had stupidly enough, perhaps, but as a precautionary measure, extinguished our light, and there was some time lost before we got a match struck. When at last our candle burned up the light revealed an empty cellar.

The lads were gone. They must have contrived to pass us, as there was no other way of exit, and they had not left even so much as the candle end behind them. They had feared, no doubt, that we were the police, or at least unfriendly visitors, and the instant they heard the noise, extinguished the light, seized the cards and crept, glided, crawled—melted away, in fact, it seemed to us, so quickly and silently was their exit performed. We examined the cellar. It was nothing but a low dark dungeon apparently unused except by outcasts as a sleeping place.

There are hopelessly degraded beings so enslaved by the drink crave that, rather than not indulge the passion, they will spend their last farthing on liquor, though they know that passing

the night out of doors will be the penalty. And
this they do not on an occasion only, but habitually. An experience with one of those pitiable
creatures will for ever haunt our memory.

Groans, mingled with short sharp sounds like
the barking of a dog, attracted our attention
as we were wandering among some untenanted
hovels, which had to all appearance been given
up wholly to the rats. Following the sound, we
came upon a scene which beggars all description.
Lying on her back, with her head upon a heap
of rubbish, was a woman of loathsome appearance. Her garments were tattered, filthy rags,
her hair was like a wild beast's mane, and foam
was gathered on her lips. She groaned and
barked, and gnashed her teeth, and rolled from
side to side as if in torture. With the stench
of the filthy den there mingled another odour
that served as an explanation of the scene. On
the floor was an empty bottle ; it smelt of
methylated spirits.

"Dynamite," the name by which that nauseous
liquid is known in the language of the slums, is
drunk when dearer and more palatable liquors
cannot be got, and by those persons whose palates
have become so depraved by spirit-drinking that
even whisky is not strong enough for their taste ;

they must have something that grips the gullet in going down. The drinking of dynamite is frightfully prevalent among the lowest orders in Edinburgh; indeed it may now be classed as one of their favourite beverages, and the ravages that it makes upon their physical wellbeing must be very great. But home, health, life itself are held at light value by the man or woman dragged along in the clutch of the spirit-demon.

Another incident and we have done with this section of our theme. It has been said that the weariest and most loathsome life that age, pain, or penury could lay on nature would be a paradise to what we fear of death : but there are cases, pitiful, pitiful cases recorded in Edinburgh, where death has been robbed of all its terrors by the horrors of life.

The same night on which we saw the dynamite-drugged woman, we came across a young woman crouching under the shadow of an archway. Her pinched and worn cheek was pressed against the cold stone wall, and when we stopped to speak to her we met with a hard, relentless gaze. It was only after a little kindness had been shown her that her stony coldness gave way, and she spoke to us in a hopeless, heartless fashion.

In a few words she gave us her whole story. She was homeless and friendless. She had had a husband and child, but the one had deserted her and the other was dead. For some months she had had a wretched existence, and had it not been for thoughts of her mother she would have killed herself ere now. She had had very little to eat, and she had fainted so often recently that she thought she would soon die. She wished she could die that night, she was so weary, and cold, and tired of living. Though her face was thin and haggard, it was easy to see that it had once been handsome, and was yet by no means coarse. When we began to show some interest in her she almost smiled, and said it did not matter now, it would only be for a little while longer. We gave what we could—she was so listless she hardly seemed to notice the gift—and at her earnest desire left her, warning her that she would probably be disturbed by the policeman on his rounds. " Oh, no," she replied, as her face brightened up for an instant. She had seen him and begged him to let her remain; he had done so, and given her a portion of his supper; he was kind and would not touch her.

Invoking a blessing on the head of the generous night-watchman, and leaving the worn
figure on the steps, we turned and went our way;
for we felt ourselves powerless to give further
assistance in such a mournful case.

VIII.

MISERY IN THE MASS—WHAT IS, AND WHAT MIGHT BE.

In putting together in the shape of these sketches some of our experiences in the slums of Edinburgh, we have endeavoured to follow out a certain plan. The conditions of life there are so varied that any attempt to describe them without, at least, some sort of rough classification, would result in utter bewilderment alike to writer and reader.

The classification we adopted was this. In "The Poor Man at Home," and the two subsequent sketches, we outlined the mode of life in one-roomed dwellings rented on the weekly system. Taking a step lower in the social scale we came to the dwellers in furnished lodgings, a class even more shiftless and improvident than the others. A step still lower brought us to the region of the common lodging-house, from which we made further descents to trampdom and the retreats of the homeless.

Each of these divisions might be broken up into many sub-divisions, every one with its separate tale of woe. Indeed, we are painfully aware that we have but touched the fringe of the subject; merely skirted the margin of this morass of misery in which so many thousands of our fellows are floundering without hope of extrication. Those persons whose knowledge of slum-life has been derived from sources other than actual contact with it, cannot summon before their imagination any accurate representation of existence there. Their general ideas of extreme misery may be vivid; but they do not produce the alternating sensations of loathing, pity, and despair that a close survey of the details of degradation arouse.

To say that the scenes are appalling is to speak with moderation. No creation of the fancy could surpass in horror the horrors of the reality; the faculty of exaggeration for once finds itself limp and over-matched. At times one can only turn away, benumbed with despair, conscious of nothing but a sickening sense of the hopelessness of the whole matter. "There is no hope; let them drift!" one is tempted to cry on emerging from those demesnes of desolation, after a night passed in threading the dark labyrinths where hunger, squalor, and vileness are met with at every turn.

Nor do these conditions pertain only to the quarters popularly known as the slums — the High Street, Canongate, Grassmarket, Cowgate, and neighbouring localities; but are to be found in other parts of the town, notably Greenside, the Pleasance, Stockbridge, and Fountainbridge, where slums may be said to be in process of growth, and where poverty and misery are none the less acute because less apparent. These also have their dreadful dens, their hordes of ragged. half-starved wretches, who live " lives that are one agony from birth to death."

But in whatever quarter of the city these rookeries are placed, their essential features are the same. The houses are foul and dilapidated, many of them a scandal to civilisation, not to mention our much vaunted Modern Athens. The people live on the borderland of want, frequently experiencing days of sheer famine, and at intervals sufferings weeks of semi-starvation. Their employment is irregular and uncertain; a "steady job" is regarded as a rare piece of good fortune. One of the commonest scenes is that of the bread-winner lying in bed, out of work and dispirited; the mother, with an infant at her breast, sitting

G

staring hopelessly into an empty fireplace, and a swarm of tattered children sitting round her and sobbing with the pain of hunger.

Add to scenes such as these occasional glimpses of barbarity and immorality too hideous to speak of, that would make the ears of the people tingle were they described in detail, and we shall have a faint presentment of the world that thousands of the inhabitants of Edinburgh are ushered into.

Surrounded by brutish associations from infancy; beaten, neglected, starved in childhood; his youth passed in society where decency is impossible, and morality nothing but a word of vague significance, the unhappy denizen of the slums is for ever knocked from pillar to post, a misery to himself and a burden to his more fortunate neighbours. Rarely does a ray of happiness stream into his life. His home-life itself is enough to cast any man into a state of perpetual depression; he has little or nothing to divert his mind from the wretchedness that encompasses him. What more natural, then, than that he should flee to the only refuge from his woes—the oblivion of intoxication! And the cosily-housed and well-fed hold up their hands in surprise and horror at the depravity of the infatuated creature, altogether unmindful, as they are, of the numberless temptations with which he is beset. If those scandalised ones realised but one-half of the squalid misery of his animal existence, they might, perhaps, join with others in the cry of pity, " In the name of the God of mercy let them pour the maddening liquor down their throats, and feel for one brief moment that they live ! "

An optimistic historian, writing on the charities of the nineteenth century, draws a picture of Edinburgh so entirely delightful that one would imagine the golden age foretold by Edward Bellamy had already arrived.

"Edinburgh," says this writer, "has a vast hospital in which a poor man who has fallen under disease or accidental hurt receives the benefit of careful nursing and the highest medical skill. Lest his recovery should be impeded by the impure air and defective nourishment of his own home, a residence some miles out of town is provided for him during the glad days of convalescence. . . . There are several institutions in which medical advice is given gratuitously to the poor regarding the manifold ills to which they are heirs. . . .

"One association establishes lodging-houses, where the very poor can live in comfort free from the allurements of vicious companionship. Another employs its resources in improving the condition of the poor by every device which Christian thoughtfulness suggests. Another watches over the destitute sick; and to the kindly words of its agents adds an open-handed dispensation of comforts which are so needful in sickness and yet so often unattainable. . . .

"The moral interests of the poor are cared for with an enlightened zeal which is beyond praise. Children who are without guardianship are snatched by merciful hands from the perils which surround them, and safely bestowed in institutions where they are taught simple industries and receive a wholesome education. In the early stage of a boy's industrial development, one society sends him forth to polish the soiled boots of pedestrians. Boys who love, or think they love, the sea, are sent to a training ship. For agricultural aspirants a farm school is provided. The government of these institutions is entrusted to some of the wisest and best of the citizens of Edinburgh, by whom unwearied personal care is given to the interests of their unfortunate clients. Women who have fallen from virtue are sought out and gathered into an institution whose influences are directed towards their restoration. Criminals, whose term of punishment has expired, are taken charge of by a society whose agents find for them honest employment and consequent deliverance from the temptation to commit fresh offences. . . .

"A vast machinery, worked with noble devotedness, seeks to carry the light of religious truth into the dark places of Edinburgh. . . . Nearly every Christian congregation has selected a district, where its members visit the lapsed poor, and strive to awaken, in hearts dulled by suffering, some interest in the magnificence of eternity. . . .

"This disposition to raise the fallen, to befriend the friendless, is now one of the governing powers of the world. Every year its dominion widens, and even now a strong and growing public opinion is enlisted in its support. Many men still spend lives which are merely selfish. But such lives are already regarded with general disapproval. The man on whom public opinion, anticipating the reward of the highest tribunal, bestows its approbation is the man who labours that he may leave other men better and happier than he found them. With the noblest spirits of our race this disposition to be useful grows into a passion. With an increasing number it is becom-

ing, at least, an agreeable and interesting employment. A future of high promise awaits that
community whose instructed and virtuous members occupy themselves in carrying to their less
happily circumstanced neighbours the good which
they themselves enjoy." *

What a splendid fairy tale! What bitter irony!
To one haunted by the spectres of slum life,
this description of a poor man's elysium must
read like a masterpiece of sarcasm. He may
spend his days and his nights among the hovels
of the poor, and yet not discover anything but
the most shadowy traces of the working of this
mighty organisation.

Yet this romancing chronicler is not altogether
a fictionist. He describes our charities as they
are on paper. We have, in truth, this magnifi-
cent and costly machinery at hand, but how much
disorganised, mismanaged, abused, the wail of the
little ones, the grievous voices of wearied women,
and the deep curses of men struggling for existence in the dark places of Edinburgh, will tell.

There probably never was a time when the
desire to raise the poor from their miserable

* "The Nineteenth Century, A History," by Robert
Mackenzie.

condition was stronger in the hearts of the people than it is now. That the public are ever ready to loosen their purse-strings in such a cause the number and wealth of our charitable institutions are sufficient proof; and everyone who knows of the vast labour spent in those obscure places by hundreds of "noblest spirits," unknown to the world and unmindful of its recognition, will feel assured that willing hands would not be lacking.

Of money there is enough for present purposes. Of charity-mongering there is more than enough: the people are in danger of being demoralized by ill-considered charity.

What is needed as a *first step* in the direction of the condition portrayed by the historian we have quoted is the combination and organisation of the numberless charitable societies which are working assiduously and faithfully, but independently, and without knowledge of each other's movements.

It is time to have done with this guerilla warfare, to abandon this irresponsible skirmishing, and to attack the evil with united front. Not till then shall we see any appreciable amelioration in the conditions of life in the slums of Edinburgh.

PRINTED BY
TURNBULL AND SPEARS
EDINBURGH

SCENES & STORIES

OF THE

NORTH OF SCOTLAND

BY

JOHN SINCLAIR.

Illustrated with Three coloured Character Sketches, and
Eight Views of Scenery.

OPINIONS OF THE PRESS.

THE ACADEMY.—"A more enjoyable and thoroughly Scotch book than this has not been published for many a day. Mr Sinclair has at his command a wonderful treasure-house of racy stories of ministers and ministers' men, and of hundreds of other 'worthies' and 'characters.' He is also one of the most enthusiastic and successful of Scotch landscape-painters in words. Mr Sinclair's volume is the most successful Scotch book that has been published since Dean Ramsay's Reminiscences, and even to that book it is in some respects superior."

NORTH BRITISH DAILY MAIL.—"The book has been written, its author tells us, with a three-fold aim : to awaken interest, to stimulate, and to amuse. That it will accomplish each of these purposes does not admit of a doubt ; the scenes described are out-of-the-way, and Mr Sinclair's description of them is bright, racy, and vivid, adding human interest to graphic delineation."

THE GRAPHIC.—"Some of the stories and accounts of queer characters are very amusing. The illustrations are good."

NATURE.—"Mr Sinclair has produced a book which may be read with pleasure."

Edinburgh : JAMES THIN.

THIS IS THE ORIGINAL ESSENCE.

A CUP OF DELICIOUS COFFEE
CAN BE MADE AT A MOMENTS NOTICE
BY USING

T. & H. SMITH'S
ESSENCE OF
COFFEE WITH CHICORY
known to the Trade as the Finest Brand.

MANUFACTURERS OF COFFEE ESSENCES
SINCE THE YEAR 1840.

MR JAMES FAIRBAIRN,

Superintendent of the Grassmarket Mission

(UNDENOMINATIONAL),

is willing to conduct any reader of "Slum Life," whose interest may have been aroused by reading the book, through the scenes therein described.

Mr FAIRBAIRN has so many calls upon his time, that he must ask all who intend to make a visit to the Slums, under his guidance, to subscribe £2, 2s. to the General Relief Fund of the Grassmarket Mission.

Cheques should be made payable to the Treasurer, Mr R. T. SCOTT, 26 Queen's Crescent.

Mr Fairbairn has conducted the following Gentlemen, amongst many others, through the Slums of Edinburgh :—

> The EDITOR of the late "Daily Review,"
> The EDITOR of the "Evening Dispatch,"
> A former EDITOR of the "Edinburgh Evening News,"
> Professor T. D. SIMONTON, Astronomer to the U.S.A. Government,

and

The AUTHOR of

"SLUM LIFE."

Communications regarding appointments, to be addressed— JAMES FAIRBAIRN, 12 Antigua Street, Edinburgh.

JAMES FAIRBAIRN, Advertising Agent, 12 Antigua Street, Edinburgh

16th June 1891

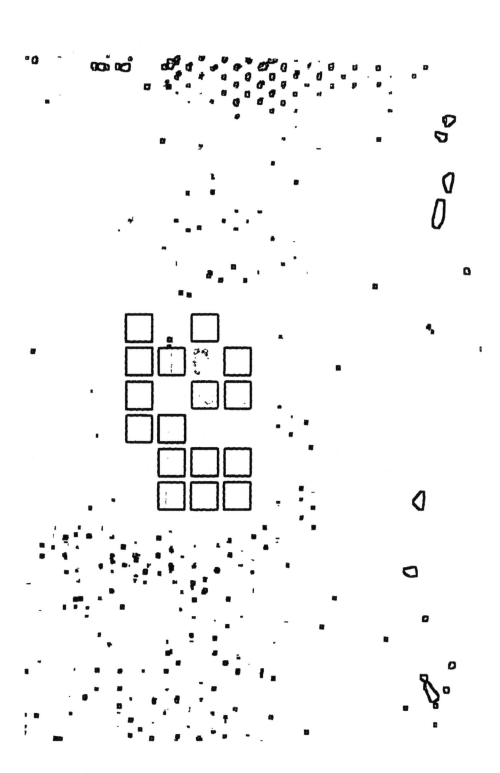